MW01228842

C.H.E.A.T

Step By Step Guide To Mastering The Art Of Cheating,

Yup, Cheating is a form of Art!

One Hit Wonder

Literary Art

C.h.e.a.t

My Inspiration

For Nikiva Laquana Banks

a.k.a First Lady Wonder

If it were not for my lovely wife, I wouldn't know what it is like to be "LOVED UNCONDITIONALLY" and would therefore be unable to reproduce the effects thereof for the masses.

It truly has been worth suffering through all of the "failed attempts" of the past to know that I have finally gotten right at last! I will forever Love You the same (If not more). My Beautiful,

QUEEN!

I'm bout to CHEAT that ass

under the table for LIFE!!!

Your KING,

One HitWonder

C.h.e.a.t

Table of Contents

Super Big Special
Thanks

A SUPER BIG SPECIAL THANKS to my LORD and SAV-IOR and my silent partner in making this all so possible! If I were to ever believe that there was an event in my life that GOD had predestined and prearranged with his own two loving hands other than my Marriage, the very same Divine Appointer knows that it was the day He introduced the Banks family to Yours!

I look forward to many sound, fruitful endeavors and the process (blessed process) of making a lifetime friend and sibling in the faith. May God bless you, your writing, your publishing house, your marriage, (Hi Mike) and your home in more ways than you have been a blessing to mine!

Forever Indebted,

One Hit Wonder

and CO.

C.h.e.a.t

Special thanks to MyOneHit actual artist Daya Banks

Here you go my Love! Your "True North"

when it comes to dating (so much later in life) and

knowing if you are "Truly Loved".

May you find the MOST CHEATING KING on the planet!

Love Dad

C.h.e.a.t

C.h.e.a.t

INTRODUCTION TO

C.H.E.A.T

Would you believe me if I told you that there was a way that you (A Man),could effectively cheat on your partner (hopefully a Woman), in a way that she would not only respect but love you for? "Absolutely no way!" That's what you are probably thinking at this point and I sure as well don't blame you. I mean if there were actually a clown that smooth, they'd probably bottle him up and sell him in shots.

Well my brothers, lets get the packing process underway because I am the one and same fellow and if you pay very close attention to what I am about to say, break down, process, then internalize the information as I relay it, I am fairly certain that when it is all said and done, you too will have mastered the Art of Cheating.

Cheating has always been the most vile, the most heinous, and the most spiteful thing that one lover could, can and more often than not, does to the other. In most "discovered cases", it's usually the male. But I just get this nagging suspicion that the female brain may actually mature faster than the males, which only semi-confirms my theory that y'all have been doing it under the radar since the first infidel act. But since our feeble minded self's haven't caught the majority of y'all "yet", I will continue to place the burden of guilt at the feet of the less academically inclined species and fellas that just so happens to be us, when it comes to this matter and not this matter alone. Just admit it clown so we can move on!

Now that we are no longer in the denial stage (Don't Even Know It's A Lie) we can finally make some progress and with just a little effort on your end, we may be able to end the negative stigma that our unfaithful, two timing, adulterous ancestors (no disrespect, what's done is done) left us in and shine a new positive light on the way that we cheat on our wives, girlfriend's, baby mama's, and boo's for the remainder of time.

So please bear with me as I single handily try to usher in a new paradigm where we as men can be praised and our women will be pleased every time and may actually encourage us to cheat and fall deeper in love the more that we do. Crazy Right? Perhaps, but I'm willing to bet that some smooth brothers like us can pull that off with room to miss.**If you with it, LETS ROLL!**

C.h.e.a.t

Chapter 1

T

I hope I don't lose anyone with the tactic that I chose to use in helping our mission become a success.

I tried to choose the least complicated route but when dealing with something so delicate, unstable and complicated as God's gift be glad this skit aint written in hieroglyphics.

I chose to use the word cheat as an acronym, as well as the blue print to mastering the one and very same art. Yes, Yes, Yes! Cheating is absolutely, positively a form of art and when done in the right setting and upon the right canvas, with the proper utensils, a master piece is almost always going to be the result. Having said that we are going to work the letters in reverse from **T** to **C** in order to get a more thorough working knowledge of not only what we are doing but why we are doing it at all. So, without farther ado lets begin with the letter **T**.

The letter **T** in **CHEAT** means *"Treat Her Like A Queen."*

There is a saying that goes, "The same thing you did to get her, is the same thing that you have to do to keep her." Fellas, after 39 years of living and fumbling my way through one relationship after the other, I can honestly sit here and write to you that the clown that ran that skit was obviously gay. Because any dog worth his bones knows that the monotony of the same old every day tedious life will make a chick jump ship quicker than you can say "Wait chick don't jump!" So it is imperative that you keep things fresh, exciting, and romantic like your relationship depends on it, because it does right here in this gap. Especially if you're reading this.

Most men will actually have no idea where to begin when it comes to treating a woman in such a manner. I'm not putting any of my brother's down at all so don't get it twisted or misconstrued. The only reason any of my brothers would be unable to do so is because they've never been shown how in the first place. Ladies, Y'all got to take some responsibility for the untimely death of all acts chivalrous as well. Y'all don't think so? Okay, Whose idea was it to date bad boys? So, who is it to blame when you are doing stuff, like opening your own doors, paying for your own food, and his for that matter?Who is to blame when your bodies are battered and your emotional bank accounts are drained? Sure is not the nice young man that sang in the church's choir. I'm just saying.

But be that as it may, my goal is to end the vicious cycle of ignorant men who are incapable of expressing something other than anger. It is to educate and inform my brothers on the art of wowing women and how to treat them like Queens they were created to be. 90% of the battle is in knowing your lovers love language. What that is, it's the one thing that you do for them and when it's done right, absolutely nothing says that you love them more. Some women prefer acts of service, and quality time above others. While other women are more partial to positive words of affirmation, or physical touch, and some will never feel as if you love them unless you are showering them with gifts. Whatever her love language is, it is your mission to find it out, learn it by heart, and speak it as if your native tongue. Even after we accomplish all of that, we still have so much more to learn. So, don't look at this as a sprint, but as marathon that never ends. Because there is never going to be a finish line when it comes to treating your woman like a Queen. This is a very big task my brothers, but it can be achieved in the most simplest of ways.

Just looking into her eyes and saying *"You are so beautiful"* while maintaining strong eye contact the entire time can and will (in most cases) make a visible difference the more it's done. You will see a different reaction the first time vs when you don't make eye contact. How in the hell can you not when you can actually see her? Right!

Her opinion should be solicited in even the most minute topics when conversing. By asking her "What do you think honey?" You are showing her that you value her opinion, care about what she thinks, and what matters to her. That alone will open up channels of communication that will otherwise remain locked and untapped the entire time. Being able to express her mind openly by invitation via her lover is going to inspire her to want to be expressive in other ways as well. Most women find it erotic to be placed on the spot by their men, especially when in the midst of company. There is really no higher compliment that you can give than everyone's full attention to the thoughts and views of the women that you love and adore.

Random, unexpected compliments go a long-long way (especially in public). Try waiting until you are in a crowded room or area, while socializing and say something like "Doesn't my wife or girlfriend look amazing today?" And watch her light up from within and turn 50 shades of in love right before your eyes. By drawing attention to her beauty and positive attributes you are inadvertently giving her confidence and making significant deposits in her emotional account simultaneously. That's right, double threat guy. Two birds; one stone. You can actually get so good at it that it will become like second nature to you and re-solve all of the buffering that we experience when it comes to relating to the fairer sex (in most cases). When you make a women feel beautiful both inside and out (despite her true condition) it's a feeling that not only lifts her up but it carries over to you as well. As a man (A real man), *(A real man of God)*, your pride should come in how well and how wise you allow your steward-ship to be over the things that God gave us dominion, and if you haven't experienced it yet, there is no better feeling than the good feeling you get from making your woman feel good.

At this time I would like for those of us whose minds were in or near a certain hypothetical gutter just then to rejoin the rest of us once more. Because I'm not talking bout that good feeling clown! Although that may occur, I'm talking about that feeling, that unmistakable feeling you get when the love that you have poured into her is as visible as the slight difference in her penciled on eye brows. Your light should literally shine on others through her for as long as you can generate and inspire those feelings. Simple gestures have the most profound effect! Little things like hand written notes, single roses here and there, love coupons, text messages, and calls that are unexpected, and meaningful contact (i.e. physical touch), are all small but sure fire ways to make waves in your relationship. It is always going to be the small, subtle things that matter most because they are the ones that will get noticed first when we are no longer preforming them like before.

Now don't go around telling folks that I said, "All you got to do is little things to treat her like a Queen". Nah, because I would never be so naive as to believe that or foolish enough to teach it. Even though they may go a long way, the road that we are traveling is longer and more complicated than any number years of experience can navigate so easily. But those little gestures will pave the way for your more grandiose endeavors.

This also makes it so that your larger attempts don't seem so far between when you have so many small meaningful displays bombarding her all of the time. Truth be told, our best efforts will count as nil, nothing, zero, love, and zilch if they are not genuine, not forced, constant, not sparse, timely, not out of convenience and done from the heart, not regretful or grudgingly.

In my own expert messed- up opinion, our best efforts won't even scratch the surface of the promises we've broken, the lies we've told, the trust we've broken, the pain we've caused, the love we've lost, and some wounds take forever to heal. I said that to say that, *"Unwounded flesh has no reason to heal"*. Make every second and every word that comes from your lips to her ears be just like music. Your words should be the sweetest, your tone should be the most caring and concerned when it comes to all matters her! Understanding should only be sought by you after receiving it through her.

She should feel like the most important person in the room and in your life at all times. She should see and respect you as the go between for God and herself! But you can only be seen in that light by her through loving her unconditionally.

The woman or Queen in your life has been placed under your care by God and it is your job to love, provide, protect, and lead her in a way that is pleasing to both her and our Heavenly Father. This is by no means a religious publication at all. Now having said that, I will say this,"God's love is the only love that will be sufficient enough to truly last a lifetime". So, until you are walking in the light and love of the Lord there is absolutely no way that you can truly love or become a beacon of light to her at all.

Without His love our best efforts will only cause more harm than good. My love alone isn't enough! Your love alone isn't going to cut it. Seriously! How can something as willfully strong and as stubbornly selfish as human nature be capable of loving anything unconditionally? Come on, be real! Man, the minute we are rejected or turned down for any reason at all we instantly start to develop a contingency plan and make reservations to be with someone else. Sad but true. That's really the most feminine made move that a real clown could make.

Instead of developing a plan B when something like that oc-curs, we as men should immediately go grab our mental tool kits and work like hell trying to fortify plan A. When you only have one plan it has to work! But the man with many will not see things the same. The three keys to success at **ANYTHING** are

Focus, Focus, Focus. So when you turn laser like focus on your significant other, you place yourself in the position to learn. Now all you have to do is observe carefully and she will teach you everything that you need to know about her.

Knowledge is power and with great power comes great responsibility. Getting to know your lover can be the most blessed, the most exciting and the most interesting thing that one could do. The learning process is mostly trial and error, but almost every successful person has failed their way to success. Don't be afraid to be yourself even if you'd rather be someone else. Nine times out of ten you are going to attract someone that sees only the good in you because that's all they want to see. So, it's okay to make some mistakes and drop the ball just as long as you recover nicely.

When it comes to treating her like a Queen, you must first see yourself as a King. No woman wants to be subjected to the reign of a tyrant, dictator, or oppressor for a single moment and if you can identify with any of these titles then this stuff was put together just for you. Safety and security are very high up the ladder of the things women want. When a man can make a woman feel safe and secure that man should be counted among the wise. Despite her toughest tough guy act, she is still really just a scared little girl who feels lost and alone (in most cases) and when we truly step up as men and fulfill our roles as models and men they will no longer feel the need to replace what they feel is missing and begin to relax more, ease up more, and with any luck maybe even love you more.

But until we can give them the safety and security that they desire they will always feel the need to protect and secure themselves from the defensive stand point that we should be manning all the while.

How could she possibly feel like a Queen when she is always ready for battle? How can she be made to feel like royalty when she is constantly on the front line? She may even try to convince you that she is good, that she's got this, that it's no problem, or that she may even find pleasure in that position but believe you me, it's all a lie.

Clown, no woman wants to lift a finger unless it's acquiring a fresh coat of polish. A woman literally should have the luxury of being able to choose if she wants to work or not. Forcing her to work a job or have a career to survive, provide, or support the household will cause her to develop resentment towards your lazy tail, and most of the time even she is unaware of these feelings until pop goes the weasel! Bruh, don't get your weasel popped bruh! I promise you that there is a better way. Give her the respect, attention, encouragement, and love that she not only desires but deserves daily and your weasel should be doing all the popping. One Valentine's Day after I had taken my girlfriend to work (by force) I went to the local Wal-Mart and bought some rose pedals in a bag, three long stem roses, candy, a bear, balloons, and a nice bottle of wine to go with the dinner I was going to prepare.

By the time everyone was exiting her building I had parked my Monte Carlo directly in front of her work place and was standing outside of the front door with my bag of rose petals ready. The moment we locked eyes among a sea of people, I immediately began to throw them at her feet. That alone sparked a reaction among her co-workers that neither she nor they will be likely to ever forget. One woman even commented, "Ooh, it's just like Coming to America!" I continued to back pedal and litter her work place with full, lush, red rose petals all the way to my car. The passenger seat and floor boards were covered in rose petals on her side and a giant teddy bear was in the passenger seat waiting for her with a box of Millionaire Chocolates.

Everyone was in absolute, complete awe as we drove off into the evening and I swear that I could actually feel her blushing. I continued on that night and prepared her a seafood dinner of snow crab legs, lobster tails, and shrimp scampi. But before I made her dinner, I drew her a bath. I sat on the edge of the tub and plucked the petals from a single rose into her bath water as she soaked away. After personally giving her a bath, I placed a second rose on the tray that I served her dinner from and we enjoyed a glass of Moscato as we ate.

She came to bed wearing a pink lace negligee and I spent the remainder of the night catering to her every desire on top of a bed of roses and a room filled with soft flickering candles. My girlfriend floated to and through work all that next week and her co-workers still remember the romantic stuff that red clown did for her almost 10 years ago. I literally did such a good job at treating her like a Queen that day, that it carried over into the following weeks, and I could see a visible, clear difference in the way she looked at me let alone loved me. And I did my very best to treat her like the Queen she truly was every day.

You too by the end of this will be able to woo and wow your woman and all passers by almost the same. Almost! It's really a simple formula if you see it. The more that you treat her like a Queen, the more she will see and love you as her King. Do things for her just because or for no reason at all. The more unexpected the gift the better it is (in most cases) unless she just really hates surprises. If that's the case then you are on your own! Not a mental health counselor bruh, just a clown that knows how to spot, greet and treat a Queen. **T** is the last letter in the acronym **CHEAT** but it is also the first step in the process of successfully cheating on your woman in a way that she will not only accept but respect and love you for. You just have to treat her like the beautiful, amazing, wonderful Queen that she is ALWAYS, If you really want to **CHEAT**.

C.h.e.a.t
Chapter 2
A

Every woman wants to receive the attention of someone who has eyes for only her. Too often I see men ogling and appraising other women while they are walking beside the one they love. Flag on the play! I mean really? You clowns aint even trying to hide that stuff either. Don't get me wrong, I have been that clown a hundred times (or two), but I never considered the negative effects that it could and did have on my girl and my relationship.

I wasn't doing it intentionally to spite or disrespect my girl at all, I'm just really distracted by a multitude of different shapes and sizes! That was my best excuse at the time. Sue Me! Either way, it is down right disrespectful to look at other women in the presence of your woman. There is absolutely no way in hell you will ever be able to get away with cheating if you are still behaving so recklessly and immature. The more I teach y'all the dumber I get!

Look clown, If you ever plan on getting this stuff internalized, then we gotta pick it up just a taste. If you are ever going to get good at cheating, you have to lock them wondering eyes down, and learn about the "A" in cheat. In order to get to that place where she is going to be cool with your cheating tail cheating, you are going to have to learn how to adore her and only her.

Yup. The **A** in **CHEAT** means *"Adore her"*.

When you Adore your Queen you give her something that no one else in the world has, which is all of your attention and most of your time. Whether you believe in it, or not, female intuition is spot on 99.99% of the time. So when she goes to noticing the little thing that you no longer do for her like before, that is all it will require for her to go on a hoe stroll like never before. Please believe me son, after she reaches that point it's all down hill from there. Down hill doesn't have to be your destination though my brothers. Lucky for you, there is a better way.

When you truly adore her it will show. She will know, see, and feel it all across the board. Even her demeanor will seemingly be 100% in tune with yours. Adoration is not the same thing as admiration at all, though they are closely related. See you can admire someone and turn around and admire someone else in that same setting. You can admire multiple people, places, and things all day, every day until your admirer breaks down on you, but rarely will you be in the same place with two people that you adore at the same time. Allow me to expound a bit more on exactly why I feel like that.

When you adore someone you only have eyes for that person and that person alone. Everything about her will either interest or intrigue some part of you that can't resist the urge or fight the hunger to know more. It's crazy, but real as this pandemic. Even the little, silly, trivial, boring, things that are one day gonna make you run a hose from the exhaust to the interior will seem like the most fascinating thing that you've heard since ears. But that's the beauty of adoration.

When you truly adore her she will feel as if she is being appraised every moment that she spends in your line of vision. I can already see some of those mice making y'all's little wheel's move already, so I'm going to slow this chapter down just a bit for a sec because we aint got nothing if we don't have an understanding.

Peep this my brothers. I was walking through the grocery store with my pregnant girlfriend one summer because she was craving pickles and peanut butter or some thing like that. As we were entering the building a couple of ladies were making their exit.

Both of which ladies were wearing tops that had to be painted on, and shorts that exposed cheek on both sides. I only know this because I have 20/20 vision and my peripheral was on point that day as well Oh, and hindsight. I think I have hindsight. I could already feel my girl side eyeing me like James Evans off Good Times trying to see if I was going to cut my eyes or turn my head their way.

I don't know what it was or why, but for some reason I got the feeling that she thought that I really wanted or was going to. She must be a psychic or some thing because just as sure as she thought it, I did it without thinking. But before I did, I grabbed her by the hand and as my head began to turn in their direction I began to say, "Baby, I sure am glad that you love yourself and I enough not to dress like that. Besides, even if you did, surely you would make them take those back to where ever they got them from. Cause they aint got nothing on you. I gave her hand a squeeze and kissed her lips.

Now here is the part that is going to shock you!

I was telling her the undisputed truth. Were those other girls hot? Smoking! But what they were not, was my girl. See even pregnant, swollen, bloated, moody, and not looking no where near her best, I was still able to be honest on my answer simply because I adored her. I had been internalized her value and her worth to me long before that day. So, when facing that situation, I was able to keep my eyes on the prize. The woman that I adored!

After that she started directing my attention to the booty shorts and coochie cutters that other woman would be wearing and say, "Baby, nah she ought to be shamed for wearing that mess. But do you think I would look good in that?" Now, I get to say things like, "Way better than her baby. Look, She doesn't even have a big enough butt to strain the fabric." Then we laugh and she gives me a playful punch to the arm and I give her a nice slap on her butt and we go on our way together.

Everyone knows when someone adores them. It's too easy not to miss. You will usual catch them doing stuff like staring off into space while looking in your direction. You will always see them smiling this goofy smile. They are usual super helpful and will always be ready to assist you with World War Z if that's what it came to. My very first real crush or feelings of love was for my high school sweet heart. A girl named Natholie Hood. I mean back then I was really in love for real cause I knew what it was at thirteen. Nah, maybe not love, but I knew how to adore. I would tell her that I loved her and she'd just say, "I know". When I asked her how she knew she told me, "Because of the way you look at me. No one has ever looked at me the way you do!"

If the eyes truly are the windows to the soul then I saw her soul more than her. Those big, soft, brown eyes were the focal point for me and I didn't care about getting lost at all. I have no doubt in my mind that I adored her and she in her heart till this day know that to be true. Even though we did not go the distance, I can assure you that the entire time we were near all I saw was her.

That type of immature, innocents is the very essence of what love represents, but it is not always going to flow like that. Sometimes you are going to actually have to work at it and work for it, if you think it's worth having. You are going to have to find something to like about the stuff you don't like about her, if you really and truly adore her. When a man adores a woman that man becomes gentle, kind, caring, and attentive making him what's known as a gentleman in deed. He will go out of his way to bring her comfort and do so more exceedingly and in abundance.

Make sure that you are the type of man that is going to be a blessing to the type of woman that she may or may not be. Besides, if you are not a blessing then you are a curse, or even worst, a plague. And you are only going to do more harm than good. Because if you truly adore someone then you will want to give them the very best version of you to adore in return. There is no greater return on such an investment. They say that the, "Highest form of admiration is imitation". But I beg to differ. In my eyes the highest form of admiration is adoration. The art of having eyes for only her.

Another commonly used lie is, "Nothing lasts forever." In order to see the untruth in that, you have to first get a clear understanding of what forever truly symbolizes. Often way too short of a time that we have on this planet in this life is just about forever as it gets as a human being. Your forever begins when you are born and your eternity begins when your forever ends. Now that we understand forever, we can now begin to form a vision of not only acquiring but maintaining something for the duration of that period of time.

Hopefully by now, you are thinking "Queen",and not pit bulls or some other neander- thoughts (i.e. primitive way of thinking). Because if any of those other things can gain your adoration above her, then brother you need a shrink! How could we not want our most valuable and most precious resource to be lavished upon our partners?

Our time and attention is what women have been vyiing for since our untimely discharge from The Garden of Eden. And believe you me, the more of it they get the better off you will be.

You should never enter your Queen's presence out of anything but the pure desire to do so. Because anything else will only send negative vibes and wave lengths that she can decode and decipher just by breathing the same air as you. Anything other than desire is going to drive an even bigger wedge between you two and your tempers will flare. But when she feels that you simply can't and don't want to be away from her, things will still eventually flare up, but the only thing smoking will be the two of you after she cums.

To adore her means to engage in a completely selfless act. You literally begin to think of her more and of yourself less. You are going to be more interested in what interests her and more happy for her accomplishments than she will be. Thoughts of how to add value to her and enrich her life will consume you and soon she will be the center piece for your life and new relationship. Even old relationships can be reborn, but only If the two can ever begin to adore one another. Any two people who have ever truly adored one another are probably still making babies today!

So, to give you a leg up in the adoration game my more educated clown's, I'm gonna break the word adore down into really easy steps that are fool proof. So ADORE is now about to become a five step acronym as well to help oil down that dry cheat crap y'all passing for game. So your lady will have no doubt in her mind that you simply adore her when you are proficient at A.

The **A** in adore means to *Anticipate* her needs, wants, wishes, and desires.

If you've been paying her any kind of attention or have spent any real quality time with her at all, then you already know more about her than you realize. Since you met her, she has been showing you almost everything that you need to know about her and her demeanor. You may have been missing the signs and I'm sure it's only because you never knew they existed. I'm already hip. So let me take the time to now hip y'all before they ship y'all green tails. Look at and listen to her even while she sleep, and the more you are willing to do so the more she will reveal, and most of it without trying or even being aware. It's just all up to you to gather these bits of info and put them to use. Put together a play that is so new, so smooth, and so you that she will think you read her mind or some thing when all you ever did was read her. Presenting her with what she needs before she is out or asks for more will only speak volumes to her about how much she stays on your mind.

The **D** in Adore means *"Defending"* her.

You must also defend your woman from all things big, small, foreign, and domestic. "Defending" a woman's honor is not only a pantie dropper, but is also the ultimate man move. Especially if you get your butt kicked (in most cases). Sympathy sex is dope, but hero sex is da bomb clown, so I suggest you bob and weave. There is another saying and this one goes, "To the victor goes the spoils." The victor in this sense is going to be the victorious one, aka "The winner". The spoils are also known as the spoils of war (i.e. treasures or booty). So the victor goes to the booty!

Hopefully nothing can be of more value to you clowns than that beautiful Queen that is looking to you for guidance, substance, affection, protection, and love. Anything else make's you blind, dumb, and gay. Real gay! So she is going to be your spoils. Hopefully you will be the victor and would have won any battle that you ever engaged in for her honor. Once again, defending your woman is the ultimate man move. Every woman wants to feel safe and secure in the arms of her man. The better you are at protecting her, the safer she feels, and becomes more in love with her strong, loving, protector of a man. She will literally come up with creative new ways to express her gratitude for keeping her safe, sound, and protected from all of the bad, bad people in this world. Hint, Hint.

Moving right along on into step three which is represented by the letter **O.** In any relationship that has any real chance of lasting, both partners have to communicate openly. Effective communication is open communication.

So the **O** in adore means to *"Open communication"*.

Because it is the only way anything can be achieved. When the lines of communication remain open the relationship as a whole will flourish like no other. Information is the blood flow of any business, organization, family or relationship. We all know what blood's occupation is within the body. So it's no surprise at all when I tell you that without it's life giving blood the body DIES! Yup. Kicks the proverbial bucket just like anything else. Relationships included. Hell, that goes double for relationships!

The moment the two of you stop openly sharing everything with each other is the moment that you give open invitation for lies, and deceit to start moving in, and once they get settled in, it's all over. Once the initial lie is introduced, the fabric of that relationship becomes stained and strained even till the point of termination and sometimes that involves life not just relations. So the next time you decide to bite your tongue, hold your peace, let her find out for herself, or just plain ole forget to tell her something, try to envision what would happen to your body if it's life force (i.e. blood cells) were to hold back on flowing for an hour or two. Hell, Lets make it the whole day then. That's

what you need to see or at least try to make yourself see before the very same pointless death steals the life and love from your home and relationship alike. The ONLY way to prevent that from happening is by being open and honest at all cost. I don't think anyone in their "right mind" is going to avoid the company of an honest man.

And on that same note, there isn't a single woman in the world who will continue to tolerate a liar and a fool. For some reason women (in most cases) react less harsh to cheaters than the men they know to be incapable of telling the truth. The truth is the best gift you can give your woman in this day and age in my (once again) expert messed- up opinion. We should all know what truth does by now. Some are you are going to make the statement "Set you free," but nothing can be further than the truth.

The truth was intentionally designed to get someone screwed up, for screwing up and 95% of the time that will unmistakably be you. However, in the other 5% of the times that it actually does "Set you free," or at least takes the focus off of you, there is absolutely no better feeling in the world. Even if it hurts! Pain only endures but for one night, and then joy comes in the morning. She will forgive you for One Million mistakes but she will never forgive or forget you for telling one lie.

It aint no secret that relationships and secrets do not go hand in hand. As matter of fact, they don't belong in the same room. EVER! Man I implore you my brothers with hope in my heart and tears in my eyes to work hard at keeping the channels of open, effective communication healthy, and constantly flowing. Because if the blood flow and death scenario wasn't enough to at least create a desire to get better at communicating if nothing else, then, you might already be dead my brother. If that's the case then I can't say "I told you so, can I"? You have to work hard to keep your lines of communication open and constantly flowing between each other on even the little inconsequential stuff. I'm serious! The more you communicate about nothing, the more proficient you become at communicating about everything. When you get to the place where you can do that the things like secrets, lies, skeletons, and the likes are uprooted like weeds and cut out like the cancers they become. So keep on talking my brothers. Allow there never to be moment of silence whether comfortable or un. Silence has done all of the real violence in our homes and relationships today.

It is really imperative that you begin building or rebuilding those broken bridges. And if I were you I wouldn't waste a lot of time doing it because we never know how long we actually have to do this in. I personally find it exciting to be racing against my own clock, but I would never rush or race against hers. Take the time to talk daily together in person. Face to face will always be the best way to talk, you just have to love one another enough to be willing to. So until you get those lines open, don't expect much else to. This is a major key in how well you will do when it comes to relating to His best work. We won't get all of this down in one sitting my brothers, so don't overexert yourself trying to figure it all out right now. Rome wasn't build in a day, and women are way more complex than Roman Architecture.

All things worth acquiring are usually going to be done one day at a time, one second at a time, and one moment at a time. So I am more than confident to write to you that if you apply that same process to your efforts at communicating with your woman like never before, the next time you cheat on her, you will be all that she is able to talk about in a positive light. All you have to do is adore her daily and repeat the process over and again. Before you know it you'll be finishing her sentences.

All we have left to learn when it comes to the art form known to us now as **Adoration,** is what the final letters represent and how we can put them into play in a way that will maximize our return on this (long-term) investment that we are about to make. The last two steps are really how we will maintain and keep up the condition of what we are about to gain.

The final letters and steps in how to **ADORE** your woman are the letters **R** and the letter **E**.

The **R** simply stands for *"Repeat"*.

That just means to redo the same thing over, and over again and again. Anytime you do something repeatedly for a certain amount of time it becomes a habit. Continue in that habit and it becomes second nature. That is something that you are so used to doing that you can do it without even having to signal your brain into action.

Your second nature will then manifest itself into a way of life. To be **ADORED** by anyone is one of the best ways to live this life.

The **E** is, you guessed it *"Everyday"*.

Repeat these steps everyday for as long as she is yours my brothers and she will always be yours (in most cases).

Having eyes for only her isn't going to be as easy as I make it sound in a world full of harlots, home wreckers, and whores. But clown I promise you a Queen in the home beats a hoe in the streets 7 days, 4 weeks. Hell, the more you make it a sanctuary for her, the more it becomes a Kingdom for you. Happy wife, happy life! That's some bull crap too! I'm just saying.

Your wife can only contribute to making your home and family happy. What life throws at us is out of our control and happiness is not external. So you are the only one who can determine how happy your life is going to be. NO ONE ELSE! Treating her like a Queen and truly adoring her is going to take effort and it is going to be work, but like any job well-done, the reward, return, and respect that you will receive from a more than grateful spouse will truly surpass that of material possession or monetary value.

Persistence is the key in this gap! You have to be just as relentless as you were when you were after her now that you have her. It's not time to ease up my brother, it's time to clamp down. FOR LIFE! EVERY SINGLE DAY! The day you don't feel like it or don't want to treat her like a Queen is the very same day you need to move on, because that is the day you will no longer deserve her! ADORE THAT WOMAN MAN!

C.h.e.a.t

Chapter 3

E

Alright, alright, alright my brothers, we are approaching the half way mark with this chapter, and since it's the chapter in the middle of the book, I found that to be right in line with the location of our next lesson. Every Queen deserves special, special, special treatment. I don't know about y'all clowns but when I want to do some special times three stuff for the Queen in my life, it's usually something that I'm extremely good at and I know that she will go nutts over.

The letter **E**, in this acronym means

"Eat The Cookie".

I know my gutter minds are elated right now, but hold your blood flow bro, because this erotic lesson is for information purposes only. So down boy! Down! Ok, where was I? Right! Eat the Cookie. I don't think I know a single male who is into women that does not eat the cookie. If you just so happen to be one out of A Billion Clowns that does not view her cookie as a culinary delight, then forget everything you've read so far, put my manual down, and go take an extremely long walk off a dangerously short pier, because aint no saving you!

Yeah, this book is fool proof not retard resistant. You can treat her like a Goddess all day my bother, but you will always be expendable to her and she will always be next to his if you don't eat her cookie. Any woman who doesn't desire her sweet, delicious, warm cookie to be eaten either A) She has never had it done, B) She has never had it done right, C) She doesn't have a cookie at all!) I'm just saying.

So if you are that extra rare brother bruh, it sucks to be you. Hopefully I can coach you away from these neander- thoughts about not doing so, but I won't waste a lot of time trying. On God, I have left clowns before. I'm not good at quoting the bible and all, but I believe that in it we are instructed to not with hold our bodies from our partners. We are to please them as we want to be pleased. Not the exact words, but there!

When you withhold something from your partner that they desire (especially sexually), you then create more unrest within your relationship than you realize. You also open up the door for a world of other unwanted events to transpire. You smell me? NO? Well what about this? There is another saying that I allowed to stick with me over the years for I guess this very reason."What one man won't do for her another man will!" That's right y'all! That is true! I wish I could discredit that in some way or another but I'm probably the clown who started that one my brother. My bad! Truth be told, that use to be my demonstration. I need to take this time to introduce myself. My name is Mr. Leroy Kendall Banks aka *One Hit Wonder,* better known to your girl as Jodi. That's right, Mr. do what that clown wouldn't do in the low down flesh.

I've only had to stumble through a few relationships in my days because I've only tried it a few times. The majority of my life, I lived it as a bachelor (no-pad) who specialized in missing pieces. What I mean by that is this, "Whatever the missing piece was in her relationship when we met up, was the only thing that I was there to provide". I have to tell y'all too, y'all clowns trippin! Do you know how many of y'all's women this tongue could have held captive? You wouldn't believe me if I told you, besides, I've lose count. Sue me! In 98% of my encounter's with unsatisfied women, it was because their dude refused to either eat the cookie or his game was totally whack (i.e. terrible). Not knowing how puts you above not at all any day. You can be saved if you are willing to learn but if not please return to page 23 of this manual and follow the set of detailed instructions that are given in the next to last paragraph.

Nothing is more sexually frustrating to a woman than not being able to reach the highest peaks of ecstasy through the avenue she prefers most. That avenue is not the same for all woman. Hell, for some women it's not an avenue at all. No matter if it's an avenue, street, cul-de-sac, highway, or boulevard, you have to learn that, like the back of your hand and be ready to roll at her demand. Catchy right? Truer words have never been spoken. To be honest, this manual is a reproduction of my personal experience gained through picking up or plugging in y'all missing pieces. Sad but true.

I know, I know, that's some messed up crap to admit and it's a dirty job that I was stellar at doing. Over the many years and my countless encounters, I kept my brothers in mind and carefully documented and stored information from every single rendezvous. I logged and stored that information so that I could one day reveal to my gender the many unnecessary mistakes we make when it comes to women and give them a solid, sound, fool proof tool that they will be able to use to hopefully undo some of the relational damage that we as men and the men who've proceeded us have caused and give birth (hypothetically) to a new era where the man is honored and encouraged to cheat.

The majority of relationships that have ended at the hands of infidel acts only ended that way because one partner withheld something that the other partner desired, and said partner became interested in someone they knew to be proficient at what was being withheld. All that means is this, "A clown wouldn't eat the cookie for his girl, and she was salty about that. She screwed around and met Cookie Monster and now that clown is beating his dick"! True story! Don't end up beating your dick bruh! You don't have to beat your dick bruh, (unless it owes you money). Lucky for you my brothers, there is a better way (Unless you are just super fond of your dick!).

Eat the cookie in this chapter doesn't strictly bind you to performing the act of fellatio, better known as oral sex, head, dome, three meat treat, slobber nikki, throat, mater, beak, grill, brain, top, etc. etc.. It symbolizes humbling yourself before and to a weaker creature in a manner so selfless and so sacrificial that it will alter how that creature sees your real true strength. Because it takes a strong man to lead from behind the crowd no matter how large or small it may be. She will experience a change so dramatic herself after witnessing both (ocular and physical proof) of your declaration and dedication to her, that I bet the neighbors will know your name.

Letting her experience you truly cater to her wants, needs, and especially her sexual desires when it means you have to go against your own set of rules, standards, codes, or laws cements in her heart and in her mind that you truly will do any thing and risk everything to please her in every way. Believe me, Clown! When a woman cements that in her heart and in her mind you might as well send a mold of your dick to them hoes, because it's the last that they will see of the real thing. Women rarely feel as if a brother will give them his last bite of food or something. So you know how it goes down when they lock some thing like that in.

Even if I were strictly binding you to preforming all of those interesting monikers for that one ecstatic act, a clown should be more than willing to entertain her southern smile for as long as it takes. I personally find it to be a delicacy or like to imagine it as forbidden fruit. Something about eating things that have been forbidden that just makes them irresistibly sweeter than usual. I wonder where I get that from? Hell, clowns should be happy that a woman wants his hot mouth down there at all.

Y'all gone wake up one day. Clowns just better expedite that process before they let me back out! For real my brothers, I can make y'all ears bleed with all of the stories I've had to listen to about how bad y'all clowns are in bed, between legs and at head. I can honesty admit that I'm so good because you are so bad. Literally! But all of that making up for y'all's short comings (no pun intended) over the years made me so seasoned and so experienced that my fiance now says thanks. She is very appreciative of all of the hours of training and experience that she will get to enjoy over and over again. In my once more expert messed- up opinion, the real issue at hand is self! Most men go into intimate arrangements with one thing on there mind, THEMSELVES! They are usually so caught up in their own wants that they are unable to provide the needs of their partner. A man with his woman at the top of his list will rarely if ever cum first. In fact, he will make it his mission, no honor, to see that ecstatic, spent, pleased, stare off into space in her eyes before he even consider his own sexual gratification. I will even go a step further and say that he may even actually eat the cookie until she cums first before even entering inside of her at all. I know I did.

I could profoundly expound on so much and so many different points under the banner of this particular topic but why beat a dead cat? I'd much rather eat a sweet, delicious cookie instead. And if you knew like I know, you'd drop everything, run home, pick up your woman and sit her directly on your face and eat away. Because I'm willing to bet you (and I'm a gambling man 4 sho), that if you haven't been eating her cookie that the flavor aint no secret. A brother knows what her cookie taste like bruh, that clown just aint you! And don't go home and jump on your woman talking about I told you that a clown was eating her cookie either. Make sure you tell her that I said you should have been that clown the whole time! No one in this world is going to hold themselves to all of the standards we set in place to so-called regulate our lives. Truth be told, we are going to break our own rules, laws, and lower our expectations every once and again. So who better to go against your own grain for than the women you love and adore?

Think about it like this. Out of all the withdrawls you've made from her emotional bank account, don't you feel the need to make a deposit big enough to replace what you've withdrawn and cushion her account? Eat the Cookie! Don't you want to take her around the globe without leaving the room? Eat the Cookie! Don't you want her to elevate to new heights, Yet get as close as she can be to you? Eat the Cookie! Eat the Cookie, EAT THE WHOLE COOKIE!! It doesn't get more clearer than that, and if it did you wouldn't see it anyway. So hopefully this has been of value to you and if I've successfully convinced one person here today to give her the world and go down on his girl, then I think this day in prison was well spent. Now don't let me get out and y'all still bucking on licking that split and I'mma steal your girl. Just playing baby! You know I only have eyes for you. Just trying to scare these clowns straight. For real though fellas, we are in last place. Women will be running this and y'all will be taking forever to get ready if y'all don't step up to the plate, bat, and wheel. I say y'all because I'm secure. I'm only hers, shes only mine and her cookie won't be missing no meals. Y'all clowns aught to thank her for being secure enough, cool enough, and thoughtful enough to not only give me her permission to hip y'all by using my past relationships, and events but giving me her blessing as well. Y'all owe Nik one, I owe her One Million! That is why this publication has been created in your honor so that other women may receive honor through how you've enriched my life.

I Love You!

Leave the cookie out for me tonight...

C.h.e.a.t

Chapter 4

Cookie 101

This brief tutorial is just a compilation of tips that I will offer up from my own personal bag of tricks, and some suggestions from some people who know exactly what they would like to experience while you are down south. All right my brothers, class is now in session. I would like to welcome you all to **Cookie 101**. Hopefully by the end of this lesson you clowns will have a little something to shoot with the next time y'all are down at the range. I'm not going to sit here and write to you as if I am the illest clown at it, but I don't think any clown in the world, would be so brazenly stupid to try and instruct the world's population of men on some thing he knows nothing about, so just chill my brothers, I got you.

The first rule in eating the cookie is and always should be "Check the Pan!" What I mean by that is this….. "When was the last time you went out to eat wearing a blindfold? How long has it been since you went somewhere and ate in the dark?" For those of y'all still scratching your head and looking around, that equates to this, "Inspect the dish before you sample it"! A proper, thorough, detailed sight and smell test should be conducted before engaging in the act. Sorry ladies, some of y'all be pushing the envelope a little too far with the personal hygiene. It is some embarrassing stuff, but either way, better safe than "Syphmouth" (i.e. syphilis in the mouth) any day. Hopefully she is willingly going to comply with your wishes because for her to refuse will only mean one thing, "Desert cooch" (i.e. extremely dry vagina).

Rules to sight and smell test…..

Ruke #1. no bumps (unexplainable), bruising, swelling, discoloration, or discharges at ALL! EVER! RUN!!

Ruke #2. no unpleasant odors or too pleasant odors. Water or absolutely nothing at all are the two top fragrances when it comes to eating the cookie. Anything bad, tart, unpleasant or too pleasant are all red flags from hell RUN!!

Once she has aced your exam then it is safe to reward her like so, kiss her lips (small kisses at first, then deeper more meaningful ones). Continue to litter her frame with kisses of all shapes, sizes, tones, and texture as you slowly but deliberately deliver each kiss methodically. Begin to imagine her entire body beginning to seize up and shake compulsively as her juices turn to honey at the tip of your tongue. That way, you have already begun to en-visualize what the end of your performance should resemble.

The main thing you want to focus on is her! Her body movements, her vocal ques, the contracting and relaxing of her muscles. All of these things are going to comprise your tour guide. What I mean by that is, "It is the way you are going to learn how to please her the way she desires". Her less desirable ques will be the withdrawing from that certain touch or feel, her silence, when you are in particular areas, and the actual vocal ques that it's not going too well. Those will usually be more grunt like emissions. They won't have that pleasurable tune to the ear. Encourage her to be vocal as you hit the spot that turns her on and make her feel good in any type of way. Note, the better it feels the louder you should encourage her to be. This is going to require you to have to be able to create a place for her that allows her to feel comfortable, safe, and desired. This is going to take some doing on your part, but there is absolutely no better reward than a successful mission. Mentally note and log those areas every time she sounds off and began to service and pay more attention to those areas more often than the others.

A real good composite of wetness, pressure, repetition, eye contact, and dialogue (i.e. dirty talk), is going to fortify your game in the areas that you are weak and may be need of improvements. You can not allow any of those terms to intimidate or scare you into backing out right here because if you do then that makes you more cat than the cookie. I'm gonna have to get on that level y'all clowns can easily relate to if any of us are going to have any type of real chance in eating some cookie in the near future, especially tonight. And by the way, phone sex is dope too. So if your woman is locked up, give her the gift of a nasty, freaky call. That can go along way I swear! It may even keep them straight. Try coaching your partner into adapting the same breathing pattern as you. This can be achieved by hovering just a hairs breath above her skin, and breathing deep breaths, and exhaling slowly as you do. Focus on your breathing and the beating of her heart. She should focus on your breathing and he beating of yours. With time and focus your heartbeats per minute, breaths taken per minute should come to be around bout the same.

Some of you are wondering why you would want to do something like that? Good question, glad you asked. Due to time constraints, I will only be able to provide two. The first reason you want to think breathing patterns is, "Where do I start?" You will certainly display dominance through three many forms of control. Control of body, (both yours and hers), control of mind, control of her emotion, control of self, control of your emotions, control of your will, and control over her will.

Once you learn how to navigate her ques and her body, then all you need is a few good moves.

Move#1. Try to trace the entire alphabet (Capitalized) with the tip of your tongue on or around her clitoris. You will have to slightly obscure the hood in order to gain full access. (After completing the caps, do lower case, then cursive, trace entire).

Move#2. GET IT ALL! DON'T MISS A SPOT! Take your sweet time and be sure to lick, kiss, smooch, tongue, and everything else under the sun to her cookie inch by delicious inch and repeat!

Move#3. Invite her to the best seat in the place! Let that baby sit on your face! Allow her to safely straddle your lips and tongue and go for what she knows!

Move#4. 69! I am a Cancer and that just so happens to be one of our zodiac signs. So you know I'm proficient here. But all that is, it's "when one of you is headed north while the other is headed south but you both are going to town". Now let me put some proficiency in there for you. EASY!

Get her to the edge of the bed (head between your legs), wrap your arms around her waist, and lift (with your knees), and all of your strength. You should be in the 96 position which is only on inverted 69.

THE REST IS UP TO Y'ALL

EAT!
One Hit Wonder

C.h.e.a.t
Chapter 5
A Ceremony

Work is an important part of life and it should be fun, and rewarding. If you are still with me, then you have undoubtedly been putting in some serious work. This serious work is very much needed and we are still so far behind. The purpose for this ceremony is to reward you all for your efforts. You see, the only reason that I have been addressing you all as clowns, it's not because of your race or ethnicity at all. I called you all clowns, because of the state of ignorance that I found you in when it comes to this subject and this subject alone. So it doesn't matter what color your skin is my friends, clown is a state of mind, and that state is uninformed. Seeing as how you guys are now in possession of a certain amount of info on a certain topic, you clowns are no longer clowns at all.

We still haven't gotten to the point where we are the Kings, we were created to be yet, so I guess I will refer to you as men for now. Congratulations men! It is my honor to welcome you into the fold of men who have vowed to change the way we cheat on the women in our lives forever. It gives me great pleasure to cheer you men on and encourage you as you battle against that awkward feeling pulling at you. That feeling is whats known as Cognitive Emotive Dissonance fellas.

What that is, "It's just the strong feeling that occurs when trying to break a habit or relearn something either the right, or a different way. In your case, it would be that urge to go against everything you just learned and treat the women you love in a way that definitely suggests other wise. That feeling will pass within moments when you focus your attention on ways to please your Queen instead of hurt her. The more you entertain thoughts the more they are likely to become actions. So by dismissing all negative thoughts and replacing them with positive, loving ways to make your Queen happy, you are increasing your chances of pleasing her significantly. I am proud of every man, who is putting forth such effort, but you as men should be proud of yourselves.

Keep up the excellent efforts men, and you will begin to resemble Kings in no time. Seriously, manhood is at it's lowest point yet and if we don't step the hell up yesterday our female companions are going to end up blowing the horn while you all take forever to get ready. Men, I emplore you not to let this transpire for the sake of everything manly.

So lets kick this crap into overdrive and reclaim our rightful places as head and Kings so that our women can go back to being Queens. Because far too many Queens are running Kingdoms in this day and age, and that my good friends fallson us as men who have failed their women. I for one can no longer "willingly" sport the black eye that we have given manhood any longer! I am determined to set things back to their natural order even if it kills me, and that will never happen until we pick up the slack and give them the luxury to relax instead of our burdens to bear.

I personally plan to make it where my Queen won't have to work at all the entire time shes in my life. I will cater to her every need and more just to show her how much I truly see her as Royalty. And if we all adorne the same demeanor, the battle is already won.

So Congratulations once again men! But we aren't out of the woods just yet. Because if you've neglected your Queen like I suspect you have, then time aint on your side. So, lets get it.

C.h.e.a.t

Chapter 6

H

Most males have developed this complex that forces them to display their more tougher attributes above any other. They will more often than not be the loudest, rudest, most confrontational people that you will find. In most cases it's going to be because that person was raised to never show any emotions other than his anger and rage. He was more than likely told things like, "Men don't cry, toughen up, and stop being so soft".

This would have surely caused him to create an identity that would allow him to hide his true feelings and show only what would be accepted. In this case that is going to be his anger and ugly emotions.

The rest of the "Tough guys" are either going to be that way because they've been hurt too many times, and have become callused, or have developed it as some type of defense, or coping mechanism. So when it comes to putting the H in cheat, it's going to take some real effort for them to pull through. They may even have to become someone completely different inside and out. But they are going to do so willingly, and without a second thought, if you mean as much to them as they say (unless they tell you, that you don't mean nothing to them, then never mind disregard).

Even being the extremely rare case when that is the situation, you don't have to let it continue to be. Find Your King! There are far too many paupers in Kings positions. As long as you allow that space to go occupied by the wrong somebody, the more time you waste being treated like the Queen that you truly are by the King that was created just for you. So, stop trying to force things to workout and let them run out for a change. The unknown doesn't have to be as scary as we pump it up to be.

Staying together because you are scared to be alone is crazy. And it will never work! You are only going to end up bitter, probably battered (in most cases), and just as alone as you were in the womb (if you were not a twin or more). So, believe me when I say, "That sometimes it's best to say Good Bye".

But in those cases where splitting is not an option, and "This just has to work", then you are going to have to work equally as hard if not harder. No if's and or butts at all! My brothers, what better way to work hard than putting the letter H in Cheat. Shall we? The letter H in our acronym is going to take on many forms in this chapter. In fact, this is going to be the letter that we unpack the most because of it's oh- so- many forms.

H is going to begin by representing.

"Hold her hand,", Yupp, two ps.

I'm serious guys! Y'all clowns think I'm a sucker for love for saying something simple like that, but that's why you are paying to read the experience she tried to give you for free, that she paid to give to me. Man, just be lucky you don't live in Canada when this drop. Rude tail."Where was I?" Oh yeah, holding hands. It doesn't matter how hard she is or how hard she pretends to be guys. She is still just a soft, sweet, kind, caring soul that needs to be loved, nourished, and fed healthy, spiritual, mental, and emotional meals daily, so that she can grow to her full strength and potential in your life. The majority of the time when they fail or are failing to maximize our value (via their presence), it's usually because we let there hand go too soon or not soon enough.

Holding hands can have a much more profound definition on so many another levels. Take another one of my life lessons to illustrate the point that I wish to make here. My fiance today and love of the rest of my life Nik was in shambles when we met. Her friend at the time was running her in a serious wreck financially due to his multitude of vices. She was also dealing with some loses of family both living and deceased and she had some unresolved issues from her past that just wouldn't let her move past the past at all. She felt alone in this world and I can honestly say from my own expert messed- up opinion, that there is only one place left that people who found themselves there are really going to see as another option and that is usually at the other end of a gun, rope, knife, razor, or piece of heavy machinery.

My baby was down bad for real. It took someone to really hold her hand through the next phase of her life because unknowing to us both, things would get much worse before better days would come. Things really got dark for us at times and almost every obstacle you can think up was thrown in our path. The only way we were able to navigate our way through that darkened maze of hindrances, was step by step, day by day, and hand in hand.

I wouldn't believe it either if I wasn't still holding her hand today. The funny thing about that is this, "Even as I sit here and tell you of our own personal struggles and the battles to over come obstacles, I would be silly not to mention the fact that she and I have never seen one another face to face". That my hand has (to this moment), have yet to actually make physical contact with hers. Yupp (2ps). Starting to make sense yet? Can you see the bigger picture that is hidden behind the little ol'e letter H? I hope so because it is going to be our greatest challenge in our quest to make our women want us to be the best at cheating. So tell me how is it that I can still be holding someone's hand today that I've never ever seen before? Give up? Easy fellas, watch.

I met Nik via my cell phone while I was in The Alabama Department of Corrections. Yupp (2ps). Prison (aka) the joint, the can, down the road, the chain gang, etc, etc, you know. So, you can only imagine how much was going on around me at the time almost 2 years ago this December (2020). She couldn't pay me the money he owed and was calling to save him from the lie he had told her about his impending attack and sodomization (i.e. the act of taking ones butthole). After going from insulted, to angry, then back to inquisitive. I cleared up as much as I could without breaking the code, and I told her about the certain laws and rules I was bounded to and that talking to someone's girl was punishable by death. Seeing that she was not just hurt by what she found out about him on her own, but troubled by something much, much deeper than whatever clueless could have done to her. I asked her "could I pray for her" and did. I wished her luck and ended our conversation. I didn't sleep at all that night because something about "everything" had me deeper in my feelings than I normally would have been about a clown "running it", on his girl period. But I just kept replaying our conversation over, and over, over and hearing her voice clearer and louder each time it played. It finally stuck out to me at about 6:30a.m. It was how "Innocent" she sounded and how good her heart must have been to let it have gone so far and I felt a powerful urge to check on her. So, I texted.

She responded, and to my surprise, was doing better than I expected. But I can see why now. She is tougher than either of us "me or him", ever imagined and he was only taking her through her final rounds of conditioning before her real fight began. Having the ability to read that play from being in the game so long, I made a sound decision to take my light and momentary troubles and put them on the back burner for a while so that I could offer to hold her hand through what I know she was inevitably going to have to face, and more than likely have to face alone.

I've held her hand through it all since then (from prison). She has literally gone through the fire and has been through the flood. I mean, "my baby could have been the poster child for adversity", but almost two years, some boxing classes, a new place, a new life, a new attitude, a new outlook, and a new love in her life, Nik's emotional back account could not be more full and it will never be as low as it was before. I love to hold her hand through her walk in life. I have become so use to it that not holding it would feel like my own hand was missing at this point.

I also know the dangers of holding Nik's hand too long or at times when she needs to hold her own. By holding her hand at inappropriate or for an extensive amount of time, I run the risk of enabling her to reaching her full potential, and if she never reaches that in my care, and I can't elevate her, then I will have failed her just as much as everyone else. I can love her till it hurts, and I can protect her to death if I'm not as careful and as discerning as I have to be for the both of us. See I have to make sure that my own personal agenda and selfish desires doesn't override my morals and cognitive thinking skills so that I don't compromise the integrity of my intentions, and so that I am always part of her solution and never the source of her unrest.

Then I had to make her my personal agenda, my only desire, and my moral compass too. I had to literally drop all of the acts that I was juggling and commit to her my hand, my time, my mind, and eventually the entirely of my O- flowing heart. See I could not have made a more rewarding choice even if I chose a box that read "More rewarding". She is the gift that continues to give even when I least expect it. How many of you have heard this saying, "Let her go and if it was meant to be she will come back?" I started that too, dude. Sue me! How many of you fell for that? Be real? Did she come back? Don't worry, if she hasn't made it yet she probably took the long way or stopped at Denny's. They be having specials. If you truly love her she wouldn't want to leave. If she feels like she is truly loved by you then you wouldn't be able to suggest something like that to her yourself, because that alone means that you never did. I'm glad I decided not to just give this away. Y'all workin' a brother.

I wish I would suggest two years just go for a damn hike in the wilderness for another two years or some thing to find herself. If you got to get lost to "Find yourself ", that means I don't know who you are either and relearning your crazy tail won't even be an occurring thought. So reoccurring would be what's the word I'm looking for? Deader-than-a-doorknob! (i.e. really dead). So please find yourself before you go looking for folk's.

Choosing where and when not to let go of their hands is going to prove to be tricky as the day is long. Because your heart, emotions, and everything that you've developed for her is going to try to convince you that she's just not ready but you are going to have to test that theory against your will and emotions often.

My bride to be Nik, her one true problem that she has and always will have is her pure golden heart that I'm sure she plans to give away as well when it served it's term for her. Sorry, made her promise not to go donating it before then. And the majority of the people she knows or meets usually run over her and exploit her love for people as a weakness and a sure fire way to get what they want from her. I mean I'm not just saying this because I am about to marry her at all so, don't think that for a second when I tell you I have NEVER in my life known, met, or even made the acquaintance of someone so loving, so selfless, so innocent, so sweet, and so giving, her heart will literally give you her last.

So, I know that I have to hold her hand in all business endeavors until she has the strength and training to handle them alone. If I were to let her hand go too early in this gap then I run the risk of allowing her to make some pretty costly mistakes or hurting someone or herself, I risk allowing her to be taken advantage of or worst. So I hold her hand through those type of meetings and arrangements and let her get experience by doing the work hands on. When she has training, education, and experience, I can than make a sound, informed decision to let go of her hand.

I can also hold her hand past knowing that she is ready to hold her own and have a reverse effect. This will become a problem because she will start to depend on you to always be there to hold her hand through everything she will ever face. You and I both know that is never going to be possible. Better yet we know that to be impossible. Therefore we never want to give the impression that we will never let go of their hands. It's going to be as hard as letting the bike go on your child's first ride but to see as they continued to paddle on without falling, the more prouder you become with every rotation of their peddling feet and chain.

You have to have discernment when it comes to making your own choice as of where and when to not let go. If they are ever under the impression that you will never let go or let them fall then they may never take any real significant steps on their own without you there to hold her hand and coach her through it. Eventually you will be holding her hand through decision's like regular ranch, buttermilk ranch, or cucumber ranch? You will suggest cucumber ranch only for her to choose thousand island. It is imperative that we get this important part of cheating down cold. This is almost the most important part of what we are trying to do with this new age cheat sheet. So, be aware and stay focused on your female counter parts for the near and foreseeable future guys. I won't tell you guys anything wrong at all when it comes to this matter fellas. I truly do want us as men to reclaim our places in this world and make our Queens so happy to be loved.

I have a partner that had a wife whose job required her to travel over the states quite a bit for days sometimes weeks on in. His wife worked any number of hours in a days time and would normally be extremely too tired to do the tedious things like cook and eat after dragging herself back to her hotel room at the end of each shift. Knowing how exhausted his wife had to be and how her meals had to be unhealthy or just plain old junk food, he drove her homemade dinner meals that he had prepared individual and frozen in microwaveable containers. He made her five days worth of breakfast, lunch, and three course dinners, that she could place in the microwave on her way to the shower and remove on her way to bed.

Instead of adorning the "Out of sight", out look towards his wife, my partner made it his mission to keep her in his sight, his thoughts and his heart. He then traveled for 12 hours one way to make sure that the love of his life had something to eat that was both good and nutritious. She was just thinking about the delicious lasagna and three cheese garlic bread sticks that he usually takes all day to bake but it would all be so worth it to have a home cooked meal. Imagine her surprise when the room door bell rang and through the peephole she sees frozen home made dinners blocking out her lover but proving his love.

He literally made such a significant deposit in her emotional account by driving half a day one direction to ensure her safety and comfortablitily that he ended up staying with her that week on the road but when they made it back home the following week it was as if they had never been closer to each other. He went the extra mile to hold his wife's hand and for his efforts was very well rewarded.

Holding her hand is one of the most significant things that you are going to do for her in this lifetime. Although it can go bad when holding her hand enables her, when done appropriately and in moderation, you are also inadvertently, creating a bond that will remain binding even if everything else falls apart. Like I said "holding her hand will take on many forms in the chapter but ultimately it is going to be your responsibility to find creative new ways to hold your Queens hand when she needs it most.

I failed to do so once before and have witnessed first hand the toll not holding her hand will take on a relationship and believe me fam, it's a pretty hefty fee. It may even cost the thing you value the most Her! I failed to hold my exes hand when she decided to return to school to become a paralegal. She was already self conscious about going back to school at her age and had I not been so selfish and stubborn at the time, I could have held her hand through what could have been the highlight of her life. But she gave up on her new start because I left her to go at it alone. When she decided to give that up I guess that's when she decided to give us up as well. Our entire way of living took a blow so devastating due to my indifference to her pursuit that we never recovered from that. I couldn't see it at first but I caused that whole ordeal to transpire simply by not holding her hand. A price too high to ever pay again.

So I will continue to stress the importance of putting the H in cheat because it is a vital piece to the puzzle. It may sound like something so simple but it is really the exact opposite because of how important it is for you to remember to hold your Queens hand. It's a must! Holding her hand is the prerequisite to a happy life. And if you really look at it, that's what her hands were created for. I'm just sayin'.

So, if you ever expect to make waves with this cheat stuff, then you better get your **H** up. Holding your Queens hand is the only way to make that happen. So, what are you waiting for? Get over there and grab a hold of your Queens hand like never before and give it just enough of a squeeze to reassure her that you have been beside her the whole time, and that you always will be. We have the knowledge, power, and ability to change the way women are cheated on forever but that is never going to happen as long as we see cheating the way it's always been viewed.

It's time for a new paradigm to begin where we as men can be proud of the many different ways that we can create to cheat on the women in our lives. All that's left for us to do now is put the C in cheat and change the game as we know it completely.

Chapter 7

C

I don't know what it is, but I get the feeling that I'm going to enjoy being the face of this new age cheat sheet. I hope that you ladies appreciate the one woman in the world who had the ability to create the desire in her man to want to see all women treated as royally as I treat her. It really befuddles me to try to wrap my mind around how we could be so bad with women that they turn to one another for the affection that we fail to provide?

Nearly 90% of Queen on Queen relationships were created out of one Queen being so grossly mistreated by her should be King that she just stopped believing in or wanting men altogether. Do you understand the complete dynamics of what you just read? Probably not, so let me dummify what just transpired. 90% of the world's lesbian's are our doing! That means only 10% of the world's female population developed feelings for the same sex without being forced or pushed in that direction. If these statistics have just an inkling of the truth (which they do), then that means Manhood is damn near extinct. So we can either die off like dinosaurs or we can do this damn thing like it's never been done before in a way that it will never be done again, and set things straight for the remainder of time.

Time is an exponential component when it comes to completing our acronym. It takes time to put the C in CHEAT. With any luck, it will take you a lifetime to successfully CHEAT on the woman in your life.

Much to my surprise, some of you have already made this move, but I'm willingly to bet it was more out of dumb luck than an informed decision. But either way, those of you in this position will already have the upper hand on those of us who haven't made the transition yet.

This is also a step that I have yet to make on my own so this last step is one that a lot of us will be able to take together. Because if you really want to put the C in cheat and be the very best that you can be at it, then it is imperative that you change her last name! And now the plot thickens! You can not effectively reign as the King in her life unless you make your Queen a wife. Because that is the ultimate man move and it will never cease to be. Changing her last name will always be any true quarter backs option in the game called Love.

When something becomes yours, you then have the ability to give it an identity or a name in other words. That name begins to take on new meaning one way or another, so be sure that you are changing her name for the better. The love of my life Nik, had to find that out the hard way just like she discovered everything else. She married a man for 25 years and for 25 years he changed her name to mud. By taking on his last name she unintentionally took on his bad wrap. Every time the cops would run her tag they would pull her over and search everything! Even Nik! Male cops and all! That's how bad of a transition taking on his last name was for her. She was literally shunned and had people turn their noses up at her and their "welcome" signs to "Not welcome", because of the name she attached herself too.

So even though changing her last name will always be the ultimate man move (in some cases), it's not always the best move. So you move heaven and hell if you have to, to make sure that the name that you are about to attach to your Queen is going to uplift her instead of weigh her down. I know it must have been unbearable for her to have to endure her fall from the grace of her family's prestigious last name in exchange for the negative stigmatic change of her new one. He literally made her life worse just by adding his last name to her first. I personally forbid anyone under the teachings in this chapter from making the same mistake.

Our goal is to add value to the women in our lives. Our mission is to raise the bar, the standards, and the roof if we have to where our Queens are concerned. You don't even have to be crème of the crop to make the difference. You can literally be the black sticky stuff at the bottom of the barrel, and be better than the clown who though he was the best at it. All you have to do is reinvent yourself. This is no time to be obstinate, stubborn, or old and stuck in your ways.

This is the ground breaking ceremony that gives you the opportunity to do it all over again. Only this time you get to not only learn from your mistakes but you are also privileged to partake from mine. You have insight that it took some a lifetime to aquire right at your finger tips, and it's all up to you what to do with it all. With great power comes great responsibility and we have been in possession of both all the while.

What is the most powerful piece in the game of chess? Some of us who still experience neander- thoughts periodically will be brazenly silly enough to reply "King", but any true King worth his kingdom will tell you it would not have ever been possible had it not been for his Queen. Until you are able to recognize your Queens true power and abilities, you will never be able to enhance them. How can you add value to something you have no idea what it's worth? Hell, you have to know the full extent of your own value before you can appraise hers. How many of you have actually considered what it would mean for or do to the woman you are with to be with you before you convinced her that you are or were the one? Did you even consider what it would mean for, or do to yourself for that matter? There is a such thing as being unevenly yoked and there is nothing justifiable about it. Because someone is going to end up pulling the other person and that alone will prove to be another source of discomfort, resentment, and unrest.

The only time you should change her name to mud is if that's your name at birth (on your certificate), and even then, I wouldn't fall for that if I was her. We would have to hyphenate that with something real creative like Mud-Millions or some thing for that to fall through. Not enough of us as men really give our last names enough thought to be able to realize the weight that they will either carry or hold them down with. Make no mistake when it comes to this. How you conduct yourself and your family's affairs will determine the type of name that you will make for your family to carry not the name you receive at birth.

Even if. You are born with a last name like Mud, when it is mentioned it doesn't have to be spoken as if, From the day you are born until around 18, you have no choice but to carry whatever stigma the members of your family before you left on it. But from 18, til the reckoning, whatever your name is worth will be because of what you made it. So now is the time to come to the complete realization of what you are about to do to the woman you love. Who is she about to become by becoming one with you? If you have never asked yourself this before now then that alone is a sign that you are not ready for the final stages to Mastering the Art of CHEATING because you only get HEAT, if you are unable to effectively intergrade the C in CHEAT by changing her last name to something that she would be honored to live up to. You can actually entrap or imprison someone in an identity that they want no part of and if you are under the teachings in this chapter, I once again forbid this to be you? And by doing so once more I am now free from being liable or responsible if your King has a learning disability. Sue him! You were probably aware of his forcing round pegs, into square holes beforehand anyhow. Clearly!

So when it comes to adding value to your own last name you have to be meticulous and methodical as well. There can be no short cuts or alternative routes other than the day by day honest grind that will withstand all of times tests and more. Yet while doing so being mindful that all it takes is one immoral or unethical act to bring a stain upon your name that the cleanest dude could never remove. Therefore we should always adorn the if not me then who and if not now then when, attitude when the value of your family's name is at stake. Become a wise steward of what's really important, of something that is going to be left behind for other's to carry or be weighted down by for whatever period of time they are going to do so. And this is just for those who are born into that name so it goes double for that Queen who is undoubtedly one day going to be inducted.

What will you be inducting her to? Will it be worth the ceremony that it will take to induct her at least? After reading this manual you all had damn well better surpass that with room to change lanes. Because once you have received knowledge that you fail to use, that homeboy is what makes you foolish, stupid, and dumb. Do you want your Queen to have to wear such an ugly crown? Hopefully, your answer is "never", and if that's so then this is how to prevent that from ever occurring!

First you have to develop a sound system of morals and beliefs that you will never bend, budge, or fold on and you never bend, budge, or fold on them. Because if you stand for nothing you will fall all of the time. And usually short of everything. No woman will ever be able to find comfort and safety in the presence of an unstable, double-minded man, or minion. So what you choose to think and believe will have all the bearings on who is ever going to be willing to follow your lead. Choose Wisely!

Second, you have to walk that walk even when it hurts. To say one thing and do another is one of the biggest red flags that a man can have to pop up! All that does is suggest and (in most cases), prove that you are either a liar or a follower and not too many women are going to be in line to be led by someone who isn't leading at all. Even as leaders we always have to be mindful that we are not just foreging our own paths, but the paths for our partners as well. So it would behoove you to solicit some input from her somewhere along the way.

So many mechanics and working parts have to be synchronized before changing someones last name that it's a wonder why we do it at all. But the best decisions are and always will be informed ones, and you can other than a few closing remarks now consider yourselves informed. In order for, T-H to channel the synergy that it will take to make this work, we have to be proficient when it comes to providing the C and change her last name for the better to something that she can look forward to answering by for the rest of her life.

Like I said before "I'm sure as hell am glad that I didn't just give this away for free, but it is worth every penny.

NOW C.H.E.A.T!

Change her last name
Hold her hand
Eat the cookie
Adore her
Treat her like a Queen!

C.h.e.a.t

Get Y'all Shyt Together

Man, I just got to show y'all some real interesting stuff before I go. The following correspondence is from a woman I met on a dating site in 2018. Her profile strictly said "Prisoners Do Not Message Me!" Y'all already know I love a good challenge so I proceeded with "Hello Beautiful, that is a beautiful sun dress that you are wearing, I bet the sun hates to come out when you wear it and steals his shine." (not exact words, probably a bit less smooth than that). I would love to converse with such a lovely creation but sorry, I don't meet the criterion in your selection process. Have a blessed day and good luck!

She was so intrigued by my greeting, compliments, comparison, and dismissal that she had to know more. Especially what criterion of hers I failed to meet. On CRIP, she will tell you today that "I forced her to change her mind and listen to me, that I made her out of a lie so easy!" How was I able to do that with such little effort? The real Million Dollar question here is, how could I not when y'all out there doing silly, kid crap like this?

One Hit Wonder, (Ken),

I wanted to follow up on the whole situation with my new guy. I am truly convinced that he is a Pathological or Compulsive Liar. This guy literally lies about everything. Check this out and I know you may be able to use a good laugh. He lies about unnecessary stuff and the sad part is HE THINKS I BELIEVE THESE UNBELIEVABLE LIES.

1. *He been stabbed and went for days not knowing it and he lost so much blood that his granddaddy was the only one who could transmit him some. (Now what he don't know is I'm an undercover nerd. First of all in order for your mom or dad not to be a match one or the other cannot be the biological parent. And if your mom wasn't a match and your grandfather was.... Um my friend sounds like your granddaddy is your daddy).*

2. *He broke some guy jaw last week and the guy and his brother are looking for him. (So you mean to tell me that you want to take me out and you have three guys looking for you? Naw, fella I'm good. Bullets have no eyes. I'll pass on that. And why is it that you broke this guy jaw and they looking for you? My concerns to that are you a violent person or do you have anger management issues).*

3. *He texted me and said turn around you passed my job. (My reply was: "You sent me the wrong text" he later replies aw my bad I miss you so much that I'm seeing you in my vision. My face is looking like that, he really thinks I'm a dumb) or a car!*

4. *Another time he was like hold on I need to go into the store. (well after holding for 30 minutes I hung up. He called the next day and said that his cousin was getting beat up in the store by his mistress and the wife came in to help her and he had to keep the ladies from beating the crap out of his cousin. I said wait but at some point you had to come back to the phone and text or call would*

have been nice. He said oh my bad… the phone was sup-
posed to have been charging but it died. Little do he
know I hung up the phone, didn't die)

5. *Last Saturday night was our date night and he said that*
   he had to go get his kids and he would have to bring
   them. I said ok that's fine.(After waiting for hours for him
   to arrive he was like, my daughter didn't want to come so
   I had to take her back. I said you drove an hour to pick
   her up and you mean to tell me that you turned around
   and took her back? He said yea and when I finally got
   home and took a bath I fell asleep. I said so you drove all
   that time and not once could tell me what was going on?
   Naw fella you lying)

6. *Sunday, we was supposed to be cooking and his daughter*
   got sick and had to go to the doctor office. After waiting
   5 hours I called and he said that they just made it home
   and she wanted him to lay down with her until she fell
   asleep.(Now I am all for the kids and fatherly bond but
   again he lying). He called me the next morning to tell me
   that he left his cell phone over his baby momma house
   and had to go back and get it. Cell phones are just like
   keys, when it's time to go you are going to make sure you
   have the two in your hands or pocket).

7. *Last but not least, the last lie that was told to me last*
   night. (I asked him why it is that he only talks to me in the
   car and never when he is home? He said that his step
   sister is on a breathing machine and it runs off of a cell
   phone tower and if he uses his phone it will weaken her
   strength. (Blank face) I said you must forgot that I work
   in a medical facility and either you are lying or they sold
   y'all some crappy equipment. (Most of all breathing ma-
   chines run by electricity). So, I'm mad at this point be-
   cause he has insulted my intelligence, then I continued to
   tell him that I suspect that he don't stay alone that he stay

When I tell you that, that is only a few of the lies that has been told to me… I mean a few by far. There is absolutely no hope in dating in 2018. Then he had the audacity to tell me that I would make a great stepmom to his kids and he wants to get full custody. I said fella you are fixing to start driving trucks next month and you will be gone for over a week at a time. Who will watch these children of yours? I swear this is not for me. I will be better alone. I thought to myself let me tell Ken that I had a false alarm on this dating thing. Back to the basics I guess and I know you probably are laughing at some of the lies that he has been telling. They are absolutely ridiculous and uncalled for. At this point I will have to accept that it is never meant for me to be happy or in a serious relationship. Most men just want sex with no commitment and if you tell them you want more they back off.

Really glad you don't mine me venting. I'll write (type) you again real soon.

Take Care! Always,

Nette

See, I hope y'all don't think I was playing when I told y'all about the missing pieces get down. That scrap was 1,000! Nette went through hell with trash dudes playing on her heart. BIG TIME!

After a husband of decades left her and their daughter for another woman. If I wouldn't have stayed in her ear and her mailbox that year she told me she probably would have killed herself! I held Nette's hand through the worst part of her life so I know she will be cool with her last minute addition to my illustration on how badly y'all **NEED TO GET Y'ALL SHIT TO-GETHER**. I hope now that y'all can see that I'm just not some joke blowing smoke but a real seasoned vet on this crap. I could have controlled that woman and on my momma I can't tell y'all how many more if God hadn't given me the ability to not sexify and objectify but to rectify the broken woman that he has given me the gift to help heal. I'm Married Now! Yupp,(2ps)! Me and Nik aka Mrs. One Hit Wonder, jumped the broom during the making of this guide. I Love her! She Inspired this and I'm going to get creative Cheating on her for LIFE!

Hope this one makes THE BOOK CLUB (hint, hint). Last Time I suggest Y'ALL GET Y'ALL SHYT TOGETHER Before y'all be stuck with each other. Sausage fest!

Now C.h.e.a.t!
Change her last name
Hold her hand
Eat the cookie
Adore her
Treat her like a Queen

She Said

YES!

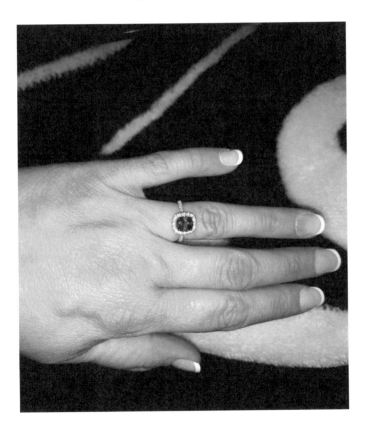

C.h.e.a.t

King Shyt

Congratulations once again Men! Or should I say Kings? You all finally made it after all. Can't lie though fam, I was a little skeptical at first, but seeing you all make it through the first ceremony reassured me that I had the right group of men all along just as I suspected. So, you all can loose the clown suits and try this King shyt on for size. Fits like it was made just for you, huh? That's because it was. That Kingly shyt that you are undoubtedly feeling right this moment will only occur twice in every Kings life, and those times are usually before, during and/or after his first sexual encounter and when he actually realizes his almost full potential and adornes his King Shyt!

So if there aren't any virgins present, then we've finally made it! But made it to where? Good question, and I'm glad that you've asked. We have finally made it to a place where, we can begin to relate not only to them but each other as well. We have let our pride render us ineffective for far too long. Pride is the #1 Killer of proud men. But up until this point I see no reason for any of us to have been proud at all. Especially the way we have allowed things to become so grotesquely out of order on our watch.

But one of the good things about being a King is how easily a good King will be forgiven for his mistakes versus how the subjects respond to the short comings of a tyrant or dictator. A good King will be forgiven so easily because of the human nature that he has undoubtedly displayed for those under his reign at some point or another. But what puts a King on his King shyt is his ability to inspire and bring out the best in his people. Now that you have been informed you now have the ability to actually choose, decide and relate better than before. But we all know that in order to master anything it's going to take time, training, talent, and technique, I don't have the time or the tools to break that one down for y'all right now, and I'm sure your Queen isn't too thrilled about the interruption from all of that good, good loving you been pouring on her. So, I won't be one of those who obviously don't know when to let that hand go. It would probably be easier to test that theory on Nik again today but for some reason I think she can hold her own for now. I wish that I was just as if not more confident in the ability of you men, I mean Kings, but I don't know y'all like I know and love Nik. I know that I've been there for and through damn near all that there is under the sun. I've held her hand almost everyday since we've met so our connection is as strong and as close as you can get to another without being related by blood.

Our get down (connection) is so righteous that it scares me at times. I believe we are so close because our whole love life is 100% non physical at this point (by force, ofcourse), but even so, what that has done is given us the opportunity to see each other for who we truly are. Sex and other physical gestures are great but they can also be a distraction or a diversion at times used by the other to take the attention off of their problems or negative behaviors so nothing ever gets resolved, only lost in the temporary pleasures of the flesh. See I can't just sex Nik into submission like I'm sure I could do easily truth be told. I actually have to relate to her, I have to open up, express the unexpressed and work through the adversity and uncomfortable moments without the aide of my genitalia, But being able to communicate verbally with no physical possibility at all forces one to be a bit more well EVERYTHING! A bit more open, a bit more patient, a bit more honest, a bit more entertaining the whole nine yards! Creativity won't flow fast enough when we can only operate under the one head setting.

But as Kings, your abilities are just as endless as the possibilities before you. You may have been on your shyt before this manuals debute but the shyt that you are about to be on after it's all said and won is only going to be fit for a King! Yupp (2ps). Velvet ropes are going to part, the heavens will rain down champagne, money will grow on trees and chicks gone be crying, not really, just effin with y'all, But all of these things should be transpiring inside of you (if that's what you like), because you deserve it. You've earned it, or are going to in the not too distant future. So a stupid big ups to all of you Kings for putting on your King Shyt for these Queens!

Now that you have been more than informed here today, what do you plan to do with the jewels that were just dropped in your lap? Pay them forward not back. King Shyt doesn't get any realer than that!**Long Live The Kings...**

Now
C.H.E.A.T
One Hit Wonder

C.h.e.a.t

Hard Truth

A s men we have let our culture become weak and watered down. This is mostly because we've gotten soft around the edges (in most cases), and have begun to sugar coat what was given to us in a snifter. Never being the one to present a problem without being willing to produce the solution, I am going to start breaking this crippling cycle right now by administering a real good dose of **HARD TRUTH**.

We have been set up to fail since go, but we are so shallow minded when it comes to the grand scheme of things that some of you won't truly be able to grasp this concept at all. Be that as it may, truth be told to and to the fold.

Someone tell me why is it that I have yet to meet a young man who will give his mother the credit for what he knows about women and how to treat them? Seriously! Why would it be left up to a man to teach something that he is just as confused about? Who knows women better than they do? So why is the blind still misleading the blind?

I see, we men have fumble and bumbled our way through one salty broad after another just as clueless as we were on day one. Why is that? How is it that after a couple centuries we are still just as bad at relating to women as 200 years ago? How is it that we keep failing to love and care for our women, in a way that will please and up lift them? Because they allow us to to! But why would they do something so silly as to allow us to continue that way is the $100,000 question?

Here is $100,000,000 worth of hard truth! Who in their right mind is going to teach you how to not only disarm and subdue them, but every one of their kind as well? No one that I mess with.

But FYI, man they can jump in and put an end to all of the relational buffering that we experience at anytime they choose. They choose not to though because it means given themselves away. And nobody is going to willingly surrender to the opposition. Nobody that I mess with. So if y'all haven't been viewing yourselves as the ops then y'all better wise up and I mean fast.

Think about it, when they come together, who do they discuss? When they make plans, who are they against? When they leave who is left alone? When the cops are called who does the bid? Y'all have got to be able to see your position in battle of the sexes! You are and always will be on the opposing team. How do you think the saying "keep your friends close and your enemies closer" came about? That clown knew his place and position and played it well.

How much closer can you be to your enemy than intimate? How much closer can you keep her than in your home? Having been privileged to such a vital piece of info like that we still seem to keep falling short. How could this be? SABOTAGE! I'm telling you! Helping you digest this Bitter Morsel of information about your position is going to propel you onto a whole other playing field. It still won't be even but it won't be as one-sided either. For her to teach you and lace you up on all there is to her is never going to happen willingly. Why would the gangster Crips give all of their ammunition to the bloods? Starting to make sense? For her to do that she would have to divulge all of their secrets and mystique so don't expect much help in that department.

C.h.e.a.t

Food For Female Thought

At some point in life we all are going to have to accept responsibility for the choices we've made or failed to make. While it is too easy to point the finger and play the victim in this day and age, how many of you actually understand the part that you play in all of this? How many of you truly understand the power that you possess as well? If you are totally unaware of all of your other super power, I can no longer allow any woman to go unaware of her power to choose. Even though you may not be able to control who you fall in love with, you are able to decide how you want to be loved.

So, if you are attracting the wrong element then maybe, just maybe it might benefit you to check your appearance once more. A man is only going to go as far as you allow him to go and if by chance that happens to be upside your head (especially for the second time or more), you may want to ask yourself some silly stuff like why am I still here? If your answer allows you to stay for more then I'm just gonna call it like it is, that's the life you chose.

Anything that continues past a week time becomes a habit. Most habits become addictions and the majority of addictions become lifestyles. So ask yourselves are you surrounded by a style of living which you can look forward to waking up to? If not, then why? You are totally free to go, unless you are experiencing Stockholm syndrome or something? So, ask yourself once more,"whose choice is it to stay?" I'm just saying...

Just a little food for female thoughts

It is up to us to uncover these mysteries and secrets of our own but we have to pass that info along as we go leaving behind a treasure trove of the things we're discovered for the generations of men to come. And in doing so, we will eventually have created the Holy Graile on how to treat women the way they deserve to be treated and that's the TRUTH.

C.h.e.a.t

Final Remarks

Seriously, having my tail ogled while I pump some chicks gas and hearing things like "Mrs. Clause is the real holiday hero, who do you think gives Santa gas money for his SLEIGH! Is pissing me off to see it done to you men and said of you! Okay, I made that last one up but it should piss y'all off all the same. So can we please man the hell up once more! If for nothing else but the sake of our sons and grandsons. Hudson, you are a **KING** and you will treat all woman like **QUEENS**. TRUST ME! Papa will never steer you wrong, grow up to be a better **CHEATER** THAN I COULD HAVE EVER BEEN GRANDSON. Of this you will always have MY BLESSING AND FULL SUPPORT.

Well, Well. It looks as if you men may be cut from a very Kingly cloth after all. It's still not my place to crown you as King in any Queens life though. That's all up to your Queen to be. I promise y'all I would select only the best for us all if it were up to me but it isn't. The ball is and always has been in your court. And you are the real play maker and always have to continue to be. It all depends on the plays that you choose to make. I can assure you that if the plays that you are calling resemble any of the plays in this manual that you are heading for Championship Status.

And if you are an effective play caller as I believe you to be then you and your Queen are about to create a team most people will only dream to be a part of. All you have to do now is keep your eyes on the prize (your Queen), and never drop the ball (her heart). Funny how this has transcended into sports talk all of a sudden, but whats even funnier then that is that this stuff actually makes sense. Well I have one more saying before I go and it goes like this. "The game is to be sold not to be told." It gives me great pleasure to present to you the game at the jaw dropping price of

Told you to be Lucky huh!

$14.99 USD

$25.00 CAD

C.h.e.a.t

About The Artist

Tuscaloosa, Alabama Native

In a year that has been defined by plaque, devastation, illness, and loss of life: **Literary Artist One Hit Wonder** (through self inventory and servant leadership mentality) has gone above and beyond to create something to not only inspire the world's population of men, but also to uplift the woman they love. And with man-hood at it's lowest, most critical point ever, **One Hit Wonder** has found his **"purpose"** in life and has made it his mission to revive and restore everything manly to it's original state.

Having himself been the recipient of unconditional love. "He has also adorned the task of informing and instructing the **King** men of his gender, around the globe on how to love the **"Queens"** in their lives in the same fashion. His fast paced, power packed, highly informative chapters are sure to keep the pages and tides turning as they progress. **CHEAT** is the **world's first** and only manual of it's kind and has **PROVEN** to be a prolific relational tool that both partners can readily access and effectively use (in most cases).

CHEAT is now what's known as **"The Wave"** in relating to His best work and our better halves. So three cheers for **Literary Artist One Hit Wonder** for taking the initiative to instruct the world's population of men on how to **CHEAT** in a way that is sure to pave the way for cheaters to come!

HIP, HIP, HOORAY!

Now **CHEAT!**

Continue Reading For A Preview to **SECURITY**! A step by step blah, blah, blah

A Glimps into
S.E.C.U.R.I.T.Y

Step by step guide to securing the woman you
love for life (in most cases)

Introduction to S.E.C.U.R.I.T.Y

So in my manual titled **"CHEAT"**, I touched on some of the things that are "very high-up" the ladder of the things women want and desire. Does any one recall what the two things I mentioned were? Right! **Safety** and **Security**. The safety part I am sure I pretty much covered under **Defending** her honor from everything big, small, foreign, and domestic in the **ADORE** her chapter of **CHEAT**.

What I would like to do is break down and help you all build on, now is the secure side of that equation. To secure something means something completely different than to keep it safe. They too may be very closely related, but will never be one and the same. Don't make the mistake of thinking just because she feels safe means that you have also provided that blanket of security she needs, or because she feels secure that she regards you as her safety or safety net.

Man, I know, I know, but the problem is that you don't. But hopefully by the end of this, you too will know everything that I know (and more), about how to ensure the security of the woman you love, adore, and want to protect even from her self if that's what it came too. And one day it may come to just that (in some cases). Security has been woman's primary need since she took your rib. I'm Hip bros. I wouldn't have believed it myself either for all that tough, hot stuff, they be poppin, if I had not been privileged to witnessing that exposed with my own mf two understand me?

It's really killing me too for this to be the one thing in my life I vowed not to publish or use to help improve what's taking place within my gender or anywhere else. She honestly would never forgive me and I won't risk being the reason she has to burn in hell, because I broke a promise. I'm too good of a friend. But believe you the clown with the pen when I scribe this. She really safer than safe bruh. Loud talks, neck snaps, hand claps, even slaps are all really big gestures. That's it, that's all. Illustration. When confronted by a big bear or some other wild animal that you know for #1, is bigger than you, #2, alot meaner than you, #3, more than likely hungrier than you have ever thought about being, what is the very first thing they tell you to do?

Bluff! Bull crap him! Make him believe that you are the biggest, meanest, hungriest chick in your back yard right now and bear is sounding like steak tar tar. Get me messed- up! Bank! Seriously though. That is exactly what they tell you to do. Well, that and some other stuff, like don't turn away, look in the eyes, don't run, leave the A-1 sauce in the car. But it all boils down to one big bluff. Now who do you know in their right state of mind that is going to stay broke when they can sell a Million wolf ticket? Right. Shyt on da cool it's a clown that is terrified of you to the point of personification and he doesn't even realize that you so scared of him, that you had to out scare his tail at some point. And how might I ask were you able to successfully frighten that dude? Big gestures I'm assuming either that or a big gun, because good tail whooping are not as effective as they were when we was knocking clowns out.

Sheed, I know one clown right now that will tell you that I, One hit Wonder am the ONLY clown that used to pain him out back in da gap and that clown is in his 40's and breaking clowns jaws in ADOC as we speak. See back then, one good, good chunk out that tail to 10 years to grow back. These new clowns snap back quick. What he will never know (unless he pays $14.99), is that I was scared damn near paralysis because of his size. What blew his cover was his dialogue. I know how clowns that can fight talk. I grew up one. The things he was saying made me beat his stupid tail.

He had me going at first until he messed around and told me that "his hands were colder than a fish plate", me: "What the crap?" him: "You heard me punk". A mother freaking fish plate. Me: "You forgot your chips", and RAN IT ON EM! On God though, I almost got my tail beat for trying not to laugh at the clown. I would have normally shot up top cuzz my brother was there anyways, 2 on 1 lets do it! But I had to ask him what the crap he had just said incase he didn't hear that right. Cause truth be told, if you got a cold fish plate from "anywhere" you need your tail beat and I must have known that at 12 years old.

But lets get back on track now. By using those big, mean, scary words, and gestures, many people have been able to rescue themselves from would be predators. There is a saying that goes "it works if you work it", that's all I got to say about that saying there. So fellas lets be mindful of this chapter when we find our selves in the position of wounded, corner, animal with no way out. Try to see the possibility of how you may have gotten your-self there in the first place.

Ladies, I wasn't going to go here but I must. All men are not equally secure. There is a little game called poker y'all, and in the game of poker there is a saying and song made famous by a Mr. Kenny Rogers and it goes, "you got to know when to hold'em, know when to fold'em, know when to walk away, know when to run." it says more but that's all I wanted to give y'all. Some of y'all just plain ole holding'em too long and walking too damn slow (or not running fast enough). Either way when you do that with someone who can and more than likely will react negativity at some point, what you are then doing is what is referred to as gambling. Lets unpack this more shall we?

What is a gamble? Well just by looking at the prefix you can safely assume that there is some kind of game involved. That game in your world is the chance that you are taking by trying to scare a bear with big gestures, you playing games! But what about this game actually makes it a gamble? That is a very, very good question and I'm glad that you asked. Any game has to come to it's end in order to determine it's winner or runner up. That really only makes for competition at this point. But the moment that you part something of value at stake you then enter into a gamble and become what is known as a gambler. One who likes to take risks for gain. Monetary, or other. So in your world what you are putting at stake with those scary big gestures is well, your life. And what makes the gamble an actual gamble, is he fact that there is a possibility (small or gargantuan) that you could or will lose what is at stake and in your particular gamble the stakes are too high. All I'm saying is this… Fold sometimes! You don't have to play every hand to win, it's perfectly normal to get out of there every now and again. (Yes Ken, Listen to your own advice here bae, this is your wife commenting on this one)!

There is a very prominent saying in my city and it goes, "clown, you live to fight or play another day!" Words to the wise now. I'm telling you. That's all I got for y'alls bluffin' tails right here, right? Deuces! I really just did that to piss them off. For real men, I wanted to use that illustration in order to hopefully be able to paint just a clear snap shot of the behemoth of a task that has been set before us. Lucky for you guys, you have just hired the dopiest, locust, realest cat that there is in this business, to get y'all to the promise land. For DA unbelievably low. I'm probably the IHOP of instructors at this gap.

Be that as it may men, King-Men and all under my per, I want to be the most frequented individual when it comes to training men and King-Men alike. Because to me, it would become symbolic of my very own arrival and transition into one and the same place. "Man Hood". So, it is and is going to be my life's workand mission to restore it to it's original state. Perfect? Nope. Willing? Yup! Damned if I do, Damn Gay if I don't!!!!!

You have probably figured out in "**CHEAT**" that my training methods are a bit unorthodox but highly effective, a little rustic but understandable and 100% in-one filtered but real. So always remember this saying right here, "It's not the messenger but the message that's important". With that said, we about to ride this like we tied a belt around our wife's waist and called her, her sisters name! (Don't ever do that!)

I don't even know my sister-in-law. So, I also am a bit of a what I like to refer to as acronymist, meaning I like to use words and give them meaning that will give us a more thorough working knowledge of the world itself. Yeah, don't even try to make sense of that. Just dig this. In order to be able to teach you the ramification on how to secure your woman for life, I am going to be using each letter of the word **SECURITY** in their original order, so that I may present you with a (fool) proof step by step guide on how to secure your woman for the remainder of time.

"S.E.C.U.R.I.T.Y" is very high up on every woman's must-have list. It's right at the very top. Manhood will never see it's original form as long as we are still in competition for it with those who were created from it. How can this be? However, it can, it won't for much longer. Lets secure our ship then!

Chapter 1

S.E.C.U.R.I.T.Y

The need to feel protected has been ingrained and coded into every- single- last- one- of- our- genetic- make-up's. Babies look up to siblings, siblings look up to mother, mother looks up to father and father goes to guns and God. What are they all looking and going to one another for? That is again a good question and I once more am too glad that you asked.

Safety, protection, guidance, help, shelter, umm what's another word that will house all of those various forms of aide and assistance? Give that clown some butter got dammit, because he's on a roll! Yup, right out of my mouth, SECURITY! They are literally looking and going to one another so that they may abolish the uneasy feelings of fear, inadequacy, inferiority, or any number of uneasy, unwanted emotions.

As men, we already know how willfully strong the op's (i.e. opposite sex) can be to begin with, so we should already be past hip on what it takes for them to commit something so valuable and personal to them as the will and care for their lives over to us. Most of us don't even have the will to care for a pet so I'm more than certain that there is going to be a load of reluctance when it comes to a person. Who probably had to down play their own strengths but for the sake of just your ego alone, so how dare you not take the initiative to provide her more than enough protective gestures to make her truly feel secure? However you dare, you dare not after reading this chapter. So lets go ahead and break the ice so the info can flow freely.

There is simply no way around this one guys. If you are wanting to never have a doubt or if your woman feels secure with you then you are having to have to constantly shower her with protection! Fly, swat! Bug, zap! A spider, SQUISH! A roach, STOMP! I'm sure that your whole security detail won't be spent that way, but that is a good way to start your detail. Because in order for you to be that in tune with her and your response time to be stellar, you will have had to have been A) close by, B) Alert, C) Brave, and last), observant. All A-list celebs in the Security game. If you already putting on like that then sure could use a tutor, common sense, aint so common anymore.

If that is already your battling average then good for you. But until I get these weenier bats to cracking you stuck like chuck so park it punk. Where was I? Right, bug patrol. No, seriously, that is especially kind of focus and attention that it is going to require to secure anything for a lifetime, especially something that will leave you! Don't worry though. Sooner or later you will get hip and litter the place with sticky fly traps, bug zappers, and off. Things like that will pick up some of your lighter weight because things will get thicker, quicker.

In the animal kingdom (the jungle not the show, good show tho), the KING and reigning champion is the LION. A male LION doesn't even do the hunting, how messed- up is that? How can I feel secure when I got to go kill your lunch and dinner today? Probably what lion hoes think. But they know better than to growl under their breath within ear shot of you know who too. Anyway, the point I am going to make is this. The male lion is so good at making his lioness feel secure that he also gave them the confidence to go boldly and eat everything butt first! Did y'all see that stuff on animal planet! They ate a whole mf water buffalo tail first. ALIVE!

Y'all hoes some savages. But that is also the type of raw, unfiltered, unrestrained and confidence behind strength that could confidence that you too can give to the woman under your care. They literally must have witnessed that LION do some stuff, so ugly that all he does is eat, sleep and impregnate the pride, His life on the other hand sounds so glorious and easy dosait it? But what I have yet to inform you all on is this. Leo might live like that for a very lengthy stretch, but one day on the horizon will be the silhouette of another lion or two and that will be the day that all of that r and r had better shire like an electric nickel. Because that is the same day that his life, wives, kids, home, and all that he knows goes for grabs and it is proven whether he truly is a King or a coward.

Lions are the most possessive sob's on the face of this earth. So when Leo loses he loses big. His life is always the primary. Even if he does manage to escape with his life that will be his only constellation. Because scar is about to eat his food, impregnate his pride and kill his off springs. So, to answer my own previous rhetorical question, yup. They seen him do some ugly stuff. So now Leo has to go from sleeping 21 hours a day, eating for 2, and busting the pride up for the remainder, to looking for a sweet lion he can run it on, (i.e. searching for a victory). But up until he got exposed, Leo had cemented in the minds and hearts of the pride that a water buffalo best not raise a hoof, in an butt first Conundrum.

Men that is the type of confident and security, you can give your woman if your willing to kill a clown and eat his kids.

Lmbao! Don't eat no clowns kids bro! You don't have to eat no clowns kids. Lucky for you there is a better way (unless that's the angle you wrangle).By showering her with so my protective gestures daily, even when an inkling of imminent danger present ever, you begin to sub consciously relieve her mental anxieties' about if and how well you are going to protect her. And believe you One Hit Wonder, when I tell you that there will be several lions on your horizon ready to bust up your pride. King or Coward? What will she see?

Security should be the foundation of any relationship point blank period. It's not trust. Lie! It's SECURITY! Facts! Truth be spoken in the open, you gotta be secure enough to trust a brother and not the other way around. Security is actually the prerequisite to trust. No one just blindly trust people anyone these days. If you do then ad to vice, "foolish move". I am not telling you to become untrusting, just wiser. A clowns mouth will tell you that he has been to the moon and won't have a speck of moon dust on him. So, what does that tell you? Don't watch his mouth, watch that Clown! His feet in particular. Believe it or not, your feet are the most programmed and trained parts of your anatomy. It's all they know to do! So we have been seeing signs in their walk since we've met them that makes us either secure enough or unsecured enough to trust them or tell them to "move around."

Have someone ever pulled up on you (i.e. approached you), and you immediately get this vibe that told you to "get out of there. (i.e. not associate with person)"? Well there you go, you observed something about that person weather you could put your finger on it at that very moment or not. It probably come to you later on that day, or that week, or in a dream. But whenever you received that revelation, you probably said to yourself like "something told me not to mess with that clown, or I knew that clown was foul!" That something was your gut feeling (something most of us will have to learn not to second guess). And what kicked started that was your awareness. So it's super-safe to say "to be aware is to be alive". Need I say more?

So security has to be established in some form whether a promise, guarantee, handshake, or contract before you can trust that person to fulfill their end of the deal. In anything! Especially you, what is about to be long-term-relationship. Do we all have a more thorough working knowledge at this point on the importance and the placement on the securing of anything of value, especially the woman that you love? Well just in case.

Comments

"After Chapter three I secretly began using it as a weapon towards my boyfriend!"

Kirstie

"Reading Chapter 1, I started realizing I myself can relate to this, not just men!"

Nik's Home girl

"THANKS NIK"

Woman Everywhere

"At first this book made me think What The Hell is Nik allowing her man to do? But I had to keep reading, I just couldn't put it down and the surprise I received was WOW what a twist, LOVE IT!

Larameka

"This is DOPE!"

Fellow Inmate

"As I started working with you on CHEAT, and giving you my blessings. As your wife and Team mate. CHEAT was finally ready. After all the hard work and hours and days that turned into months came to an end and you was pleased. I was able to finally read and enjoy CHEAT and the twist got me at first, then I just could not put it down. You had me on a roller coaster, I can honestly say It's better than any book I have read in a long time. One Hit Wonder aka My KING, has out done his self, You are an Amazing, Talented, Man and I am so very proud of you!" I Love You!!

Your Wife,,

Nikiva

C. H. E. A. T

Also look for these books for more of this level (and better) relational guidance from the Astonishing works of Author Tia Stewart. "Where to take my Shame", is sure to open the eyes and avenues for women everywhere to be able to come to the place where they can not only accept the part but actually be able to move forward to the future and a brighter tomorrow, after realizing they no longer have to carry around the weight and burdens of what no longer has to be "their shame"!

Made in the USA
Columbia, SC
02 September 2024

41076349R00052